Bats

Are Night Animals

by Joanne Mattern

Reading consultant: Susan Nations, M.Ed., author/literacy coach/consultant in literacy development
Science and curriculum consultant: Debra Voege, M.A., science and math curriculum resource teacher

Please visit our web site at: www.garethstevens.com
For a free color catalog describing Weekly Reader® Early Learning Library's list
of high-quality books, call 1-877-445-5824 (USA) or 1-800-387-3178 (Canada).
Weekly Reader® Early Learning Library's fax: (414) 336-0164.

Library of Congress Cataloging-in-Publication Data

Mattern, Joanne, 1963-
    Bats are night animals / by Joanne Mattern.
        p. cm. — (Night animals)
    Includes bibliographical references and index.
    ISBN-13: 978-0-8368-7845-5 (lib. bdg.)
    ISBN-13: 978-0-8368-7852-3 (softcover)
    1. Bats—Juvenile literature. I. Title.
    QL737.C5M38   2007
    599.4—dc22   2006030881

This edition first published in 2007 by
Weekly Reader® Early Learning Library
A Member of the WRC Media Family of Companies
330 West Olive Street, Suite 100
Milwaukee, Wisconsin 53212 USA

Editor: Tea Benduhn
Art direction: Tammy West
Cover design and page layout: Scott M. Krall
Picture research: Diane Laska-Swanke

Picture credits: Cover, title page © Solvin Zankl/naturepl.com; p. 5 © G. Ronald Austing/Photo Researchers, Inc.;
p. 7 © Jeff Lepore/Photo Researchers, Inc.; p. 9 © Carsten Peter/National Geographic Image Collection;
pp. 11, 15 © Dr. Merlin D. Tuttle/Bat Conservation International/Photo Researchers, Inc.; p. 13 © Dietmar Nill/
naturepl.com; p. 17 © Stephen Dalton/Photo Researchers, Inc.; p. 19 © B. G. Thomson/Photo Researchers, Inc.;
p. 21 © Tim Laman/National Geographic Image Collection

Printed in the United States of America

1 2 3 4 5 6 7 8 9 10 10 09 08 07 06

Note to Educators and Parents

Reading is such an exciting adventure for young children! They are beginning to integrate their oral language skills with written language. To encourage children along the path to early literacy, books must be colorful, engaging, and interesting; they should invite the young reader to explore both the print and the pictures.

The *Night Animals* series is designed to help children read about creatures that are active during the night. Each book explains what a different night animal does during the day, how it finds food, and how it adapts to its nocturnal life.

Each book is specially designed to support the young reader in the reading process. The familiar topics are appealing to young children and invite them to read — and reread — again and again. The full-color photographs and enhanced text further support the student during the reading process.

In addition to serving as wonderful picture books in schools, libraries, homes, and other places where children learn to love reading, these books are specifically intended to be read within an instructional guided reading group. This small group setting allows beginning readers to work with a fluent adult model as they make meaning from the text. After children develop fluency with the text and content, the books can be read independently. Children and adults alike will find these books supportive, engaging, and fun!

— Susan Nations, M.Ed., author/literacy coach/
consultant in literacy development

Look at the night sky.
What is that? It is a bat!

Most bats rest or sleep during the day. Some sleep in caves. Some sleep in attics or in trees. No matter where they **roost**, most bats hang upside down when they sleep.

A bat is a **mammal**. It has a furry body like other mammals, but it also has wings! Bats are the only mammals that can fly. When bats fly at night, they hunt for food.

Most bats eat **insects**. Many insects fly at night, too. As bats sweep across the night sky, they gobble up hundreds of flying insects.

11

Vampire bats feed on blood! These small bats bite sleeping animals, such as birds, but not people. Then the bats lick the blood that comes from the bites.

Some bats eat fruit. These bats have large eyes to help them find food. Most other bats have poor eyesight but good hearing. They use sound to find food.

The bat makes high, squeaky sounds that move away from it in waves. The **sound waves** bounce off of objects around the bat and send sounds back to the bat.

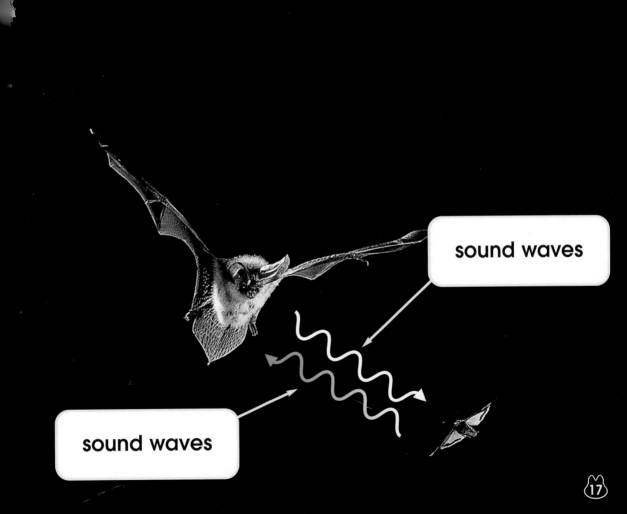

sound waves

sound waves

The sounds that bounce back tell the bat where the objects are. Using sound this way is called **echolocation**.

sound waves

Echolocation keeps bats from bumping into things — and each other! It helps bats be night animals.

Glossary

attics — areas on the top floors of houses, which are usually used for storage

echolocation — sending and receiving sounds to tell where objects are located

insects — small animals that have six legs, a body with three parts, and, usually, wings

mammal — an animal that is warm-blooded, has fur or hair, gives birth to live babies, and makes milk in its body to feed its babies

roost — to perch or settle down to rest

sound waves — energy moving through air that carries sound from one place to another

For More Information

Books

Amazing Bats. Seymour Simon (SeaStar Books)

Bats. Joelle Riley (Lerner Publications)

Bats and Other Animals with Amazing Ears. Susan Labella
  (Children's Press)

The Life Cycle of a Bat. Things with Wings (series).
  JoAnn Early Macken (Gareth Stevens)

Web Site

Just for Kids: Batty About Bats
dep.state.ct.us/burnatr/wildlife/kids/kpbats.htm
This fun Web site includes facts, photos, and a game
about bats.

Publisher's note to educators and parents: Our editors have
carefully reviewed this Web site to ensure that it is suitable for children.
Many Web sites change frequently, however, and we cannot guarantee
that a site's future contents will continue to meet our high standards of
quality and educational value. Be advised that children should be closely
supervised whenever they access the Internet.

Index

About the Author

Joanne Mattern has written more than 150 books for children. She has written about unusual animals, sports, history, world cities, and many other topics. Joanne also works in her local library. She lives in New York State with her husband, three daughters, and assorted pets. She enjoys animals, music, reading, going to baseball games, and visiting schools to talk about her books.